"At ResultMaps, we help businesses hit their targets quarter after quarter, so I love how *The MSP Handbook: QBR Edition* drives the conversation. MSPs would benefit from learning how to engage in conversations that frame them as a strategic partner, rather than a vendor."

—SCOTT LEVY, *ResultMaps*

"This book is worth more than its weight in growth. Having worked with this dynamic duo in various projects and roles, I have watched them find success by eating their own dog food... following processes and being open to suggestions and change to build profitable companies."

—SEAN LARDO, *Economy Evangelist, ConnectWise*

"Finally... the book I have been waiting for. I love how Marnie and Juan so easily distil how to drive the QBR conversation and how to have deep meaningful and strategic conversations with customers about their IT. If there is only one book you buy this year, make sure it's this one... even against mine." ☺

—CHRIS TIMM, *PSA and RMM Expert*
Sondela Consulting Limited

"*The MSP Handbook: QBR Edition* is chock-full of wisdom borne from experience. It's a strategic book, but it's also full of practical nuggets that will help you right away. You will not only learn what a fully mature approach to Customer Success looks like for an MSP, you'll also learn how to get there step by step.

MSP owners and Sales Managers should read this book, and then read it again at least once a year. Mature MSPs understand that QBRs done right will increase client satisfaction and 'stickiness' while simultaneously turbocharging inside sales. Marnie and Juan comprehensively break it down better than I have ever seen anyone do it."

—DAVE CAVA, *Encore Strategic*

"Only 15% of MSP engagement takes the form of in-person interaction, so you have to make it count. This book will tell you how to do that through the design and implementation of a purposeful and customer-centric QBR framework, with Marnie and Juan also clarifying the massive role it plays in defining your positioning, marketing, and pricing strategies."

—BRENDAN RITCHIE, *CRO, Lightwire*

"The word 'handbook' is in the title—and this book delivers on that. It reads easily, and provides MSPs with clear action steps to improve their QBR process. I love how the authors focus on benefits and outcomes, as opposed to features. This single concept will transform the way you deliver QBRs. Definitely worth reading."

—JENNIFER BLEAM, *Owner & Founder, MSP Sales Revolution*

"Juggling too many balls? Rushed all the time? No time to actually think and create a strategy that would end up saving time? *A lot* of MSPs feel this way. If you are one of those MSPs, read this book!"

— GEORGE SMITH, *Sr. Business Dev't Manager, Augmentt*

"Save yourself 20 years of learning by the school of hard knocks and read this now! Do you have clients who don't want to meet? Do they complain (or worse yet, don't complain) that they see your QBRs as just a sales opportunity for you to sell then more stuff? Are you thinking to yourself 'They just don't understand the value we provide'?

This handbook teaches MSPs how to position QBRs as a strategic tool that speaks to the needs of your client. This sets the stage for you to truly be seen and understood as a valued partner in the achievement of their goals, not just another expense on the P&L. Applying the concepts that Marnie and Juan teach in this book will drive a transformation in your client relationships, giving you a true differentiator from your competitors so you will no longer be competing on price."

—SHAWN P. WALSH, *Partner & Senior Consultant,*
Encore Strategic

"This is the handbook I wish I had when I first started my MSP. Juan and Marnie go into great lengths to explain how customer experience will win the game in the end. This is the book that needs to be in your top 5 as an MSP to survive in today's competitive landscape."

—PACO LEBRON, *ProdigyTeks*

THE MSP OWNER'S HANDBOOK

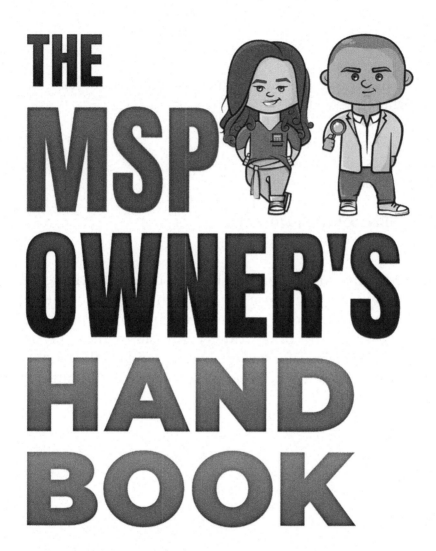

QBR EDITION

MARNIE STOCKMAN, ED.D.
& JUAN FERNANDEZ

Year of the Book
135 Glen Avenue
Glen Rock, PA 17327

Print ISBN: 978-1-64649-273-2
Ebook ISBN: 978-1-64649-272-5

CONTENTS

FOREWORD

The MSP Handbook: QBR Edition is a much-needed resource for the MSP community.

Marnie and Juan put practical and useful information together for one of the most powerful tools on the MSP toolbelt. Everyone knows the need to have meaningful interaction with clients around the services they deliver. But knowing the need versus knowing how to deliver it is a significant gap for many MSPs.

For decades there has been much gnashing of teeth around the process. It is time consuming, often clients don't make time for it, and it can feel like a useless process that doesn't provide significant value to the client—or the MSP. It is just a lot of work to check a box without bringing true value to either side of the table.

Success for an MSP through their QBR process has to boil down to two key things: simplicity and value. End customers are paying you to deliver the service they need. They aren't paying you to provide a complex report using terminology they don't understand that's overloaded with data that has no meaning to them. They want a visual report that shows how they are doing and what remains to be done.

You may be thinking, "But my MSP has this figured out." Hold on a second. The world has changed in many ways and will continue to adjust as new generations begin to take leadership responsibilities in the companies you serve. What worked (or at least appeared to work) in the past won't necessarily work in the future. *The MSP Handbook: QBR Edition* challenges the status-quo QBR thinking and offers great insight into the changes we need to consider to remain relevant for the future.

Part of what needs to happen through a QBR is to JYE—justify your existence. Why does the client pay for your services? It's no longer just to make the technology they have invested in work when they flip on the switch. Today's QBR needs to focus on business outcomes and guiding the client to maximize ROI from their technology investment.

This book will challenge the way you think about QBRs for your clients. That's a good thing, because the old-style QBR is dead. The funeral may not have happened yet, but it's coming. This book will help you re-evaluate how you can add value for your clients in a way you won't need to JYE. It'll be so obvious they'll want even more!

Don't be fooled. Your technology services are vital to your client, but delivering a value-filled QBR with business consulting guidance that delivers the client's desired outcome is worth far more.

This book can help you rethink your current process and design a QBR that clients want. It will create loyalty and stickiness unlike anything else you might do. The side benefit is it will be the sales gift that keeps on giving without you having to be in sales mode. Referrals are the natural outcome.

You'll need to read it multiple times to extract all the nuggets contained. My advice is to discuss it not only within your own walls, but with peers. That's how the original managed service model came to be—lots of peer discussions with many iterations and adjustments. But make no mistake, QBRs must change if you want to remain essential to your clients!

Remember what Thomas Edison said: "Vision without execution is hallucination." You must do more than read this book. You need to make changes and serve your clients with a better QBR!

—ARLIN SORENSEN
VP Ecosystem Evangelism for ConnectWise
Founder HTG Peer Groups

FOREWORD

Not knowing it at the time, I had the distinct pleasure of joining the IT space and Managed Services specifically at its infancy. As a result I have been able to watch our dark little corner of the channel grow into one of the fastest and most lucrative parts of the IT world.

SMBs are the largest portion of any country's economy and its biggest employer, but selling and servicing the SMB market is hard. Working with limited budgets, limited time, and tons of other "noise," it's easy to get distracted and cut corners, potentially leaving big open holes (think security) and big sales opportunities behind.

Working with MSPs and MSP business owners over the last couple of decades, it is easy to say that many of us were "accidental entrepreneurs" with a passion for technology, but not so much for the sales process, so it's always valuable to take a step back and see what we have been missing. That's exactly what Marnie and Juan are trying to accomplish with the *MSP Handbook,* and in this specific edition, the difficult topic of QBRs.

We all know we should be doing QBRs, but for the same reasons I mentioned (time and money), it's an essential step that is often overlooked or sometimes intentionally ignored. I get it. As much as you may even want to do QBRs, getting your clients on the line for such an extensive review is nearly impossible, much less knowing how and what to do when you finally get the opportunity.

This has become a critical part of the client relationship as SMB business are under attack from numerous and even more dangerous security threats than ever before. It's a scary world out there, but through adversity comes opportunity. I applaud Marnie and Juan for applying their extensive knowledge on this difficult topic. I'm confident that any MSP committed to this process will get huge value from not just this edition but the rest of the *MSP Handbook* series.

—ROB RAE
SVP Business Development, Datto
www.linkedin.com/in/robtrae

Introduction

Managed Service Providers (MSPs) spend millions of dollars every year to help grow their businesses. From consultants to coaches, peer groups to Facebook groups, and from YouTube to Zoom, there are nearly an endless number of ways to get advice on how to grow your MSP. We consistently hear:

"Develop a sales process."

"Be a strategic consultant."

"Differentiate your business."

Coaches then advise you to do this by delivering Quarterly Business Reviews (QBRs). Yet, none of that advice outlines how to deliver the QBR your customer deserves. Until now...

Welcome to *The MSP Handbook: QBR edition*. Finally, a book that will outline the why, the what, and the how of business reviews. (We will even wrestle the marshmallow of naming QBRs.)

Odds are you are an MSP who believes you should be doing QBRs–or doing them better—but:

- They take too long to prep.

- They are not strategic.

- They don't deliver value.
  (i.e., clients don't want to attend)

- You don't know what to say.

- It's just not a priority right now.

This book is a guide to help you build a bridge and get over all of that. It shares more than just the philosophy of how QBRs can become the driving force for your business. It outlines steps you can take today to deliver the QBR your customers deserve.

Whether you are starting from scratch or want to give your QBR process a facelift, give us 90 minutes, and we'll give you the insights you need to take action.

Who Is This For?

You are in the right place if you are an MSP owner, a vCIO, a Customer Success Manager (CSM), Account Manager (AM), Technical Account Manager (TAM) or any other client-facing member of a managed service or IT business. This book is for you if you know you need to do QBRs but haven't started. It's for you if you have a roughly defined process in place. It's for you if you are already doing QBRs but want some tips and tricks to improve or scale your process.

This book is also for you if you are ready to delegate the account management or vCIO/CS roles to others to scale your business and earn back some of your time. You will learn how MSPs have grown by implementing QBRs done right.

Who Are These Characters – Juan and Marnie?

You might be saying "With all of the MSP coaches and consultants, why should I listen to the two of you?"

Juan grew an MSP to $20M in six years. He now runs a vCIO school, growing MSPs every day.

Marnie runs an international software company that helps MSPs automate and deliver quality business reviews every day.

Juan won MSP *Shark Tank* on a bet that Customer Experience as a service (CXaaS) would be the future of managed services.

Marnie wrote *The Book on Customer Success for MSPs... Literally.*

So... Juan's Customer Experience meets Marnie's Customer Success.

Learn from our mistakes and learn from our wins. More than that... we have talked with thousands of MSPs. We have curated best practices and stories to share with you. These lessons will save you time, make you money, and help you deliver success for you and your clients.

The Tech: Growing an MSP IRL (in real life)

It's not uncommon for MSPs to find themselves owning a business after pursuing a technical career. That's what happened to me, Juan Fernandez, founder and CEO of MSP Growth Coalition.

As a new MSP, I learned a number of lessons the hard way. With technology now taking center stage in this new world, it's an exciting time to be an MSP or IT professional. The future of our industry offers limitless potential for those of us in this space. However, this potential often leads us down the road of trying to be everything to everyone, and there is the constant threat of commoditization.

First, a few words of caution I wish I'd heard when I was starting my business:

- It's hard to get customers.

- Success isn't just about your product or service.

- You can develop attention deficit disorder when it comes to the latest gadget or service you can sell (aka it's easy to get distracted).

- Your perception of your business and the way others see it isn't always the same.

- You are on your own.

- You won't spend all your time on the things you love, or even like.

- There is never enough time in the day.

- Taxes, taxes, taxes.

To avoid mishaps, every MSP needs to understand who they want to be in business. A combination of best practices, market focus, and customer experience can become your "special recipe." That special recipe will function as your proven process. I like to say, "The QBR is the proof that you have a process... a process that is proven." That is why I felt *The MSP Handbook: QBR Edition* needed to be written.

The Teacher: Growing CS IRL (in real life)

Not everyone stays in the same career they started out in. That's what happened to me, Marnie Stockman. After being in the world of education for 14 years, I moved to the world of Customer Success. My "customers" shifted from being high school students to school districts, and now to MSPs since I became CEO of Lifecycle Insights.

At the beginning of my career in Customer Success, I thought the objectives were clear: get our customers to use our technology (adoption), and ensure they would continue to do so (retention). The startup I was working for at the time didn't yet have a defined process or product for tracking this so I often felt like I was:

- Putting out fires
- Spinning plates
- Putting lids on pots

The company was experiencing fast growth and worked to define a process and program to let us hit those adoption and retention metrics without the 24/7 mayhem. So what did we do first? We did QBRs (and nope, we didn't do them quarterly for everyone... so rather than *Quarterly* Business Reviews, let's agree to call them *Quality* Business Reviews).

Like many folks, we did some poorly. So we learned and iterated. The bad ones involved ticket autopsies, service-level agreements (SLAs, or service-level *arguments*, as some of our partners like to say), debating over what we should be doing instead, and making a sales pitch.

As we evolved (and believe me, every QBR was debriefed and iterated on to quickly get us on the right path), QBRs turned into strategy, forecasts and roadmaps, and a focus on our client's work/goals (and how we supported them). Oh, and they also included identifying new ways we could increase our support—meaning *upsells!*

We learned the fine balance of which metrics/data to talk about and what to stop talking about, what to automate, and how to deliver a strategic conversation. The CS team and I scaled through four acquisitions from 90 customers to 900 customers and $20 million in annual recurring revenue (ARR) with the help of a process and QBRs.

And that folks, is why we decided to write *The MSP Handbook: QBR Edition*. We have seen businesses grow and scale through QBRs done right. It can work for your MSP, too.

WHAT YOU'RE GOING TO LEARN

First, you will learn that at least one of us is a nerd. (Okay, it's actually both of us.)

However, Marnie loves geeking out on great business books, so you will also learn about some great resources along the way. To start, she highly recommends Simon Sinek's *Start with Why*.[1]

In Part 1, we will give you the answer to "Why should I deliver QBRs?" We will share how this movement first started, the building blocks of a strong MSP and QBR process, and where they are now.

Once you understand "The Why," Part 2 spills the beans with "The What." Here is the tactical outline of how to plan, prep, deliver, and follow up the actual QBR. You will learn what should go into a QBR, and more importantly, what should not.

Part 3 is where you take action with "The How." Whether you plan to "cobble together" your QBR using spreadsheets and scripts or using a platform, we will show you how to make it happen.

We are glad you are still here, so let's dive in!

---

[1] Spoiler alert—If they believe in your *why*, they will buy your *what*. Simon Sinek. *Start With Why: How Great Leaders Inspire Everyone to Take Action*. New York: Portfolio, 2009.

PART 1
THE WHY

CHAPTER 1

The QBR

A critical piece to understand is that the QBR is used to communicate your value as a business consultant, not just as the helpdesk tech guy/gal. There are multiple ways to talk about value in a business. First, you as the MSP need to be introspective and look at how you value yourself.

Voice of an MSP

Twenty years ago, IT service providers drove to the offices of clients. All that changed around 2008. The housing market crashed and businesses made dramatic cuts. Remote monitoring and management (RMM) was born. The negative side effect was that MSPs lost touch with visiting their clients. QBRs were supposed to "justify their existence," sharing patch stats, anti-spam stats, and ticket close rates. But instead of seeing it as a huge savings, customers counted the costs and complained about never seeing a human being.

That was 2008—now it's 2022, and your PC will patch itself overnight... table stakes, along with anti-malware, anti-spam, and backup reports. These have become commoditized and managed services is increasingly competitive. Adding value to your client's business requires a business review that focuses on less tactical, more strategic data points.

—Alex Farling
Co-Founder and Channel Chief at Lifecycle Insights

Let's learn some lessons from Juan when he first began his MSP.

Failure and "Tuition" at the school of hard knocks

When I started my first company in the 2000s, I had a swath of ideas and general revenue forecasts, but I was missing something. I forgot to prioritize the financial side.

For my business plan, I focused on the evolving IT business needs of the day. My company had a PC repair offering, a website building division, a help desk, a server and network offering, as well as a hardware sales offering. This plan seemed solid at the time. However, profitability was not a founding principle. That was a harsh reality to face. I don't know what hurt more: the fact that I was giving away my hard work, or that I had not built a sustainable business.

Most entrepreneurs face a similar struggle when first starting—that's what makes the good ones so resilient. My mentor says, "We call that tuition—sometimes you have to pay to learn."

There is a misconception about when to implement QBRs though. Some think they need to wait to grow their business to begin doing QBRs.

False.

QBRs will help you grow from the very first moment.

Taking time to work *on the business* as opposed to just *in the business* is vital for growth

> *Adding value to your client's business requires a review that focuses on less tactical, more strategic data points.*

and scale. Focus on your stack along with pricing and profit to save some of the "tuition."

One of the values of strategic QBRs for your business is they help increase customer alignment to your stack and standards of best practice, thereby increasing profitability along the way. Knowing these things allows you to drive the right conversations with your clients. Developing a strong QBR process will help you do just that.

Value vs. Cost

On the surface, QBRs appear to cost you money, but in the real world they align tech stacks to make you efficient, solve more problems, and sell more projects, products, and services... ultimately paying for themselves.

Another common quandary early-stage MSPs share is defining their value proposition. Misidentifying a "less is more" option as a value is a trap many have fallen into.

While getting my business off the ground, I thought my value proposition was that I could do a better job at a lower price since my business was small. Well, I was right, and customers loved the low-cost options. However, this business model was not scalable or sustainable.

I was forced to look at other service delivery types to offset the sacrifices of low-cost options. Ultimately I realized that low-cost was not a business advantage. I had devalued my skills in order to win business. In the end, I had done myself, my employees, and my customers a disservice.

From this experience, I learned an important lesson. In business, you'll make mistakes. You'll sell bad deals. You'll lose money at some point. But you can catch these mistakes before they force you to drop out of business.

The client QBR cycle has as much to do with assessing your own health as it does the satisfaction and success of your customer. Use this time to recover from mistakes you have made and to learn to avoid them in the future.

Here's a list of best practices for new MSPs to consider:

- Align the client with your stack.

- o As your stack changes, make agreement adjustments along the way.

- Keep your gross margin at or above 50%.

  - o Review margins after every QBR.

- Right-size your customers by addressing growth as part of your value vs. cost conversation.

- Measure and analyze data to ensure you're on target.

  - o Adjust course early to ensure you can recover from underpriced agreements.

Most importantly, don't be afraid to change your pricing.

One of the most common mistakes experts see MSPs make is not charging enough for their services. When MSPs debrief later about having raised prices, it usually ends with them saying they lost almost no customers, and wish they'd been confident enough to do it sooner.

There is a saying:

> "You can be good, cheap, or fast. Pick *one*."

Value equals "good." "Good" equals profitable. Pick good.

Protect Your Business

In preparation for every business review, make sure your company is in a defensible position should something happen to one of your clients. You need to protect your business by being able to survive such a loss.

You also need to recognize that by offering everything under the sun, you can easily fall away from your area of expertise, stretching yourself too thin. As an MSP, there are legal ramifications to offering services that are not in your wheelhouse. It is paramount to understand concerns around liabilities, exposure, and other legalities. When you add services beyond your current capabilities or expertise, if you don't follow through on your commitments, the potential repercussions could be detrimental. Protect your business by working within your zone of genius.

With MSP regulation on the horizon, you must review contracts and terms, ensuring that you're doing what your marketing and contracts state. The most unpleasant place you will ever find yourself is on the witness stand giving a deposition to the judge and jury on why you didn't follow through on your service agreements.

> NOTE: The key here is understanding the limits and liabilities of your contracts, educating your customers on every interaction and QBR so you maintain transparency and rapport. Remember, the goal is to have business conversations vs. technical conversations.

One of the hardest things to do as a managed services business owner is to provide something tangible to traditionally intangible services, such as time and support. Yes, it's easy to deliver a report on time spent and number of tickets resolved or remediated, along with resolution time frames... but that is a *trap!* When you position value vs. cost it often becomes a sticking point for customers since they have a hard time associating the expense.

This is where you must deliver on *value*.

> *"Deliver quality product and services*
> *for a price everyone can afford,*
> *and add so much value*
> *they can't afford not to."*

This creates a major turning point in the conversation. Everything you ever wished might happen actually happens when you deliver on Customer Success and support their goals with a QBR that demonstrates how you are delivering outcomes they desire.

These desirable outcomes include:

- Increased ROI on technology investments

- CXaaS solutions that allow them to invest capital in other areas instead of just keeping their tech up-to-date

- A competitive advantage with technology

- Empowered mobile workforce

- Increased employee productivity

When you show these types of results in your QBR, your customers will promote you to everyone they talk to.

When was the last time you had a customer say, "Our IT company didn't just save us thousands of dollars, it also increased our employee productivity dramatically with new technology that gave us a competitive advantage in our industry"?

Run toward embracing an effective QBR process and you will soon be posting that kind of praise on your website. (Hmm, maybe a chapter in *The MSP Handbook: Marketing Edition*.)

You can immediately see that *your* success is tied directly to your *customer's* success. Without *them* there is no *us*. Make the investments in your process and focus on desired outcomes for your customers. In turn, this will allow you to fulfill desired outcomes for your own business.

Become a Value-Added MSP

I know there might be a misconception that the goal is to land and retain any customer who needs IT services, however, that is incorrect.

The goal of a value-added MSP is to:

- Manage customers' environments

- Deliver QBRs that guide customers to their next evolution using technology

- Give strategic advice

- Implement best practices within customer environments to ensure they are getting the most out of their technology

- Solve business problems using technology

Design your company for profit, know your value, and set yourself up for success. If you haven't done this well in the past, use QBRs to right the ship before it's too late! Don't let customers drive you to zero... because *there is no value in giving away your services.* Customers seeking good service will pay for quality. Bad customers will take you out of business with them as they haggle for lower and lower prices.

Someone once advised me, "There will always be another MSP who is in a hurry to go out of business faster than you." What he meant was that someone will always do the job for $5 cheaper. Let them! Instead, build yourself a sustainable business around good customers who value your services and see you as a partner.

As an MSP community, we can position ourselves as a reliable option for businesses. We can become one of the most resilient industries in history, but to do so, we must have correct pricing and appropriate services. The only way to ensure we can make a difference is to still be in business tomorrow and into the future.

So, we take lesson one from Juan. We will call that "Lesson Juan." (After all, he is the "Juan and only.")

1 As you climb the mountain of growing your business, build a solution stack so that incoming revenue is greater than outgoing expenses.

The Next Lesson

Now let's talk Customer Success. We must illustrate to our customers how they will be more successful by using our program, our services, our technology, and ultimately our company. This is critical. The QBR should be about how we are working toward their success.

Steal Juan's tech tip phrase: "We deliver Customer Success through the thoughtful use of technology."

To climb that mountain together, let's break down the steps to true Customer Success. There are a million ways you could climb it, but wouldn't you rather just learn one way that really works well? Here it is.

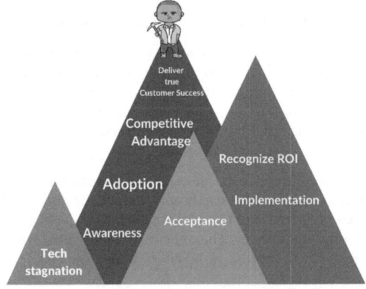

Figure 1: The mountains you will climb on the path to delivering true Customer Success: Tech Stagnation, Awareness, Acceptance, Implementation, Adoption, Recognition of ROI, and Competitive Advantage.

Tech Stagnation

Step 1: The first stage to creating Customer Success is addressing technology stagnation. Keep the conversation in the

QBR all around CS, not around the tech and most definitely not around cost. Focus on value, addressing the situation but moving quickly toward business benefits. New hardware will require less end-user friction while increasing employee productivity.

AVOID THE ROCKSLIDE

Your use of language will either help or hurt your cause. Saying things like, "This current tech is awful," or "I'm surprised this place is even running," will immediately destroy your traction with the customer.

Half of the battle is educating the end-user. This is an opportunity to get the customer to acknowledge that the present technology is not working for them, and also that they would love to have the benefits you outline.

SAY THIS: *During our assessment, we found several concerns and opportunities.*

NOT THAT: *What we found was equipment so out of date, I can't believe anyone would allow this to happen.*

Awareness

Step 2: One of the hardest things to do in a conversation is to tell someone their baby is ugly, without actually saying it. No one likes to hear bad news, and we should be very cautious. Often the negative items you want to point out are a result of a decision made by the business owner.

SAY THIS: *One of the biggest things you mentioned at the beginning of our conversation was you wanted it to just work so you could focus on growing your business. Our process and plan have been specifically*

> *tailored to provide outcomes to support you and your business.*

NOT THAT: *Since we sell uptime, we will be replacing your firewall, your router, and your access points with the latest and greatest so you have ultimate through-put, security, and connectivity.*

Acceptance

Step 3: The goal is to get the customer to trust you. With the right language and approach, you will forge a path forward together. If you can clarify the current challenges, identify what needs attention, and demonstrate the benefits they will see, you will easily move to the next stage of conversation. Just make sure you are not talking tech. Instead, focus on business outcomes and how the tech will work to improve their business and their bottom line.

SAY THIS: *In conversation with the owner, one of the biggest opportunities we found for success was increasing productivity and decreasing technology friction. To accomplish both goals, we can modernize technology platforms, which we recognize means you need a new computer.*

NOT THAT: *We are replacing your computer because you call support too much.*

Implementation

Step 4: Implementation is a key area that you need to deliver seamlessly. You also need to educate the end-user on the benefits, not just the decision maker. Get buy-in and follow up with the intended recipient. Make sure to get a statement from them on how the new technology has improved their productivity. You want to deliver those facts to the decision maker as part of your next QBR.

SAY THIS: *When we replaced your equipment, we found that it increased productivity from Day 1. We want to make sure everything we have done has continued to improve your day. Can you give me some feedback on how this has improved your productivity?*

NOT THAT: *How are things going overall?*

Adoption

Step 5: We are past the hard part. Now it's our time to prove our worth! Whether we implemented a new firewall or purchased a new laptop, the solution must be used and adopted.

> *Customer perception is 90% of the perceived value.*

Customer dissatisfaction occurs when someone feels like they didn't get what they asked for. This is no place to deviate from the plan. Ensure their success and you will enjoy yours.

MAP OUT YOUR CLIMB

Take a minute at base camp to map out the climb. Take note of anything that is unusual about where we started up the path.

We communicated that we were bringing technology that would improve the customer's business.

We gathered initial comments during implementation.

Now we need to continually follow up to see if, in fact, they are using the solution, and to learn about their experience.

You can do this though several methods. One possibility is to create a customer survey that goes out each month, asking how the implementation is going and for their thoughts around it.

AVOID ANOTHER ROCKSLIDE

Only ask questions to which you want the answers.

SAY THIS: We have successfully implemented Project Y and would like to know about your experience.

- How has the technology increased your productivity?

- How has the speed of Y changed your day?

- What is your thought around the needs of the business and the next technology you would like to see implemented?

NOT THIS: How do you feel about it?

(The latter will backfire on you, especially if their dog urinated on the carpet this morning or the office ran out of coffee filters.)

Your goal is to confirm the end-user is using the technology and is satisfied with the outcome... and that it aligns with what we said it would do for the customer.

Recognized ROI

Step 6: We have now arrived at the place where "prove it" must translate to "profits." The climb should have shown how your technology has improved the business. The customer understood the benefits and wanted to make the change. It positively impacted the business and improved productivity, resulting in additional profit. This is the moment where we can turn intangible components such as projects into profits.

It's all about how we illustrate the components. A key tip is to make sure you have tracked "total time saved" from the surveys and conversations with the end-user. You want to be able to generate an ROI report that illustrates how much the project improved the business and how much ROI the company has realized. Even small things like a new computer can generate *huge* returns on investment.

Example:

End-user previously spent 4-5 hours per week troubleshooting their computer or waiting on applications to open.

With the new computer, they not only gained that time back, but have expanded their role to take on additional tasks 3 hours per week.

Calculation

Lost time:	5 hr/wk @$65/hr = -$325/wk
Increased productivity:	3 hr/wk @$65/hr = +$195/wk
Total average ROI:	$520/wk
Projected yearly ROI:	**$27,040** (recovered employee time + add'l growth revenue)

That's a pretty strong business case for a simple PC installation.

SAY THIS: [Illustrated above] Mic drop.

NOT THAT: *I'm sure you have no idea how much time you would have been losing in product-ivity from old computers.*

Competitive advantage

Step 7: Now that we have illustrated the ROI and net benefits, it's time to start talking about how technology can not only become a profit center but a competitive advantage for your client.

In the modern age we are all tech driven. Buyers want frictionless, easy-to-use solutions. How can tech help your customer approach the modern buyer? Just like MSPs, your clients are looking for ways to improve their customers' experiences.

SAY THIS: *By implementing all of our recommend-ations, not only will you have improved internal productivity and generated additional ROI, but you will have means to support your customers in a quicker/faster way with happier employees. This not only improves internal experience but also the external customer experience.*

NOT THAT: *Trust me, you will like it.*

You can use your QBR process to help them improve their business. I call this Business Operations as a service (another topic for another handbook).

- What is the tech you're delivering doing to help support the customer's outgoing efforts?

- How are you partnering with them to help them close more business?

This is the place where you truly become a trusted partner vs. just an advisor.

AVOID YET ANOTHER ROCKSLIDE

Remember, we need our customers as much as they need us.

Example: The new security program you implemented now ensures your customers have peace of mind. It follows a security framework and all security controls are implemented to protect their data and the services you provide them.

That is a strong competitive advantage as much of the competition hasn't implemented such practices.

Make sure to remind your clients about the value of avoiding security breaches. Use ROI-based language to illustrate the potential time and financial damage of an attack.

Also make sure your QBR asks questions that help you understand the needs of your customer so you can continue to connect the dots along their success journey.

Customer Success

Step 8: This is the most exciting moment! You are able to paint the picture of success for your customer and confidently communicate the steps you successfully implemented. You will know if you have succeeded if you are able to address these steps. Trust me, your customer will be *elated*.

Don't be tempted to stop here. Communicate this win to your team and your customer. Document those steps and share that the entire team had a role in the customer's success.

2 You have scaled the mountain to Customer Success, passing the peaks of Tech Stagnation, Awareness, Acceptance, Implementation, Adoption, Recognition of ROI, and Competitive Advantage.

Congratulations, there should be nothing stopping you from scaling this same mountain with your next customer as well as all the ones that follow.

Growing the Business

Your foundation is set, so it's time to grow the business and accelerate your progress. In Jim Collins's *Good to Great*,[2] he talks about the "flywheel effect." This refers to the positive impact of stacking programs and processes to gain momentum.

Momentum is key to growth. After establishing a plan to deliver great Customer Service, the next process is to focus on Customer Success. I know, I know. You were hoping for some fun new gadget or automation. We *will* get there, but first you must focus on success—both yours and theirs.

> ### Fill-in-the-blank:
>
> My business/job is a success if _____.

Hopefully you thought big! (Aka not "I survive until Friday.") We are a success if we grow raving fans so we can help as many MSPs as possible to grow their businesses with better QBRs and Customer Success.

If you know the Lifecycle Insights team, you know we are not your typical software company. At the time of writing, we don't have a sales team. We don't do cold calls. We rarely pay for ads. Yet, we are the fastest growing QBR/vCIO tool on the market. Why is that? Because we focus on growing raving fans. These fans are our partners and other vendors in the space. We believe if we help them grow, we will grow.

If you get new business based on referrals, then I suspect you are growing raving fans, too! That is how to compound your success. If one fan tells two new ones who each tell two new fans... you get the idea. Making your customers overwhelmingly

---

[2] Jim Collins. *Good to Great: Why Some Companies Make the Leap... And Others Don't.* New York: Harper Business, 2011.

successful helps to make you successful. But you don't have to base that on anecdotal evidence. Industry experts say:

- "You can focus on Adoption, Retention, Expansion, or Advocacy; or you can focus on the customers' desired outcome and get all of those things." —*Lincoln Murphy*

- "Customer Success is where 90% of the revenue is." —*Jason Lemkin*

- "One of the best methods for retention is continuing to add value after the sale. Silence is a retention killer." —*Adam Toporek*

- "It takes 20 years to build a reputation and 5 minutes to ruin it. If you think about that, you'll do things differently." —*Warren Buffett*

So how do you turn customers into raving fans? It is clear you should focus on their outcomes and deliver value. But where do you do that? Answer: Every day in your delivery of services. But how do you let customers know you are impacting their outcomes? Answer: In QBRs! That is where you build relationships, strategize, and discuss their business goals and the value and solutions you offer to achieve those goals.

Hopefully you are beginning to see how QBRs can help you drive success. We'll dive into the components of a great QBR, but first let's take a look at the strategic relationship component.

When I first began my career in Customer Success, the goal was to develop a program that was both proactive and supportive of clients. Business reviews became a foundational component as the way to create consistent and scalable conversations that facilitate relationships and drive business outcomes.

In a world of "portals" and "notifications," this statistic struck me. In a 2020 Gartner study, SMB business owners expect approximately 85% of their enterprise relationships (of which their MSP is definitely one!) to be handled digitally, leaving 15% of the relationship to be personal engagement. The business review is the place to make this personal connection that drives the relationship.

The next question is: "Who is in charge of Customer Service in an MSP?"

> *Q: How do you turn customers into raving fans?*
>
> *A: Focus on their outcomes and deliver value.*

We get asked many times if Customer Success is a unique role in an MSP, or if it should belong to a team or the owner. The annoying answer is "Yes," "Maybe," "All of the above," or "It depends."

Regardless of the size of the MSP, there must be someone who is responsible for the role of Customer Success (CS). This typically starts as one of many hats the owner must wear. As the company grows, there will be an increasing need for an individual whose sole focus is CS. This leads to CS departments with a targeted focus. The most mature organizations have someone with a business role of vCIO as well as a technical role of Technical Account Manager (TAM).

These roles can have many names and look different based on the individual MSP. However, all are focused on Customer Success:

- Supporting your client's success toward their goals

- Reducing churn/increasing retention

- Identifying and closing expansion/upsell opportunities

- Tracking customer health/satisfaction

- Getting raving fans and referrals!

There are both strategic and tactical pieces to this work.

The strategic elements include:

- Business tech consulting
- Identifying and addressing risk
- IT roadmapping
- Budget forecasting
- Delivering on business goals

The technical aspects include:

- Tracking asset lifecycle management
- Ensuring renewals
- Preparing QBR reports
- Performing user analysis/tracking

As mentioned, this is often initially part of the role of the owner. This is the person who has the relationships. However, long-term, this is not scalable (and makes vacation virtually inconceivable).

The transitioning of roles often looks like this. The owner maintains the strategic relationship as a consultant. They hire a Customer Success Manager (CSM) or TAM to handle the more tactical elements. This role builds secondary relationships which help solidify the business relationship.

The next step is for the owner to hand over the reins to a vCIO. The CSM/TAM continues to advance the work.

vCIO vs TAM

The largest organizations have both vCIOs and teams of TAMs to support them. For the love of acronyms, we will call this entire organization Customer Success (CS) where vCIO and TAMs each play their part.

The chart below shows a typical division of labor when these become individual roles.

Let's assess where we are...

- We've started an IT business.

- We have built our stack of products and services, ensuring more money is coming in than going out.

- We are growing our business through raving fans and referrals with proactive Customer Success.

- Customer Success is the driver of growth through QBRs.

Now we are going to let you in on a little secret. Customer Success starts before your prospect is even a customer. That, friends, is how you differentiate your business.

Takeaways

Deliver the Why

Deliver true Customer Success by helping your clients reach their objectives. Share the list below at your next QBR to help your customer get a vision of the strategic conversation you will have and the outcomes you will help deliver.

	Company's Desired Outcomes	Check those that are most important to you
1	Drive growth	
2	New customers	
3	Employee satisfaction	
4	Introduction of new products/services	
5	Increase operational efficiency/processes	
6	Increase profitability	
7	Improve data collection/metrics	
8	Reduce costs	
9	Expansion	
10	Improve technology utilization	

CHAPTER 2

Why the QBR Process Is Your Sales Process

The Contrapositive (Yes, I was a Math Teacher)

If doing QBRs is "good,"
then "bad" would be to not do QBRs.

After the authors have had discussions with literally thousands of MSPs, we have learned that MSPs with a mature QBR process have been wildly successful. Those that have embraced a strategic QBR process have seen significant growth as a result. (*Keep reading for stories ahead.*) However, we have also seen MSPs that constantly find excuses to shift the QBR process lower in priority. Hopefully by now you can guess the result—their book of business remains static, at best.

We acknowledge that there are some foundational elements of running an MSP that must be addressed (like Juan's story). That being said, once you establish those foundational elements, if you are not investing in a way to demonstrate your value as an MSP (the QBR process), you are without a doubt limiting your ability to grow. Yes, it is that important.

Earlier, we mentioned some reasons/excuses for not doing QBRs. Let's review:

- "They take too long to prep."

- "They are not strategic."

- "They don't deliver value" (i.e., clients don't want to attend).

- "You don't know what to say."

- "It's just not a priority right now."

Because there are tools/platforms available to address the first concern, the goal of this book is to answer the next three. Let's chat about the last one... that QBRs are not the priority right now.

At Lifecycle Insights, we have worked with many smaller (or as Nigel Moore of the Tech Tribe would say, "nimble") MSPs who have just a few managed clients. Some have embraced the notion of a QBR process (with or without the use of our platform), while others just felt QBRs were not a priority. That of course is understandable, as starting a business is incredibly difficult! Yet time and time again, a couple of observations rang true:

1. The emerging MSPs that adopted a QBR process returned with success stories and thank you's, sharing case studies of how they have grown their business.

2. The emerging MSPs that found a way to de-prioritize the QBR process said they realize the value but just couldn't get to it. And just like anything in life, not having a plan for success is having a plan to fail. If you are not planning for your customers to be successful with your program, then you are planning for them to leave you.

The moral of this story is that you need to find a way to prioritize the QBR process. You don't need a tool/platform (although it helps). Just read the principles in this book and tailor it to your business.

There is no doubt that if your services are viable in your market, establishing a QBR process will quickly become the driver of growth.

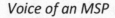

Voice of an MSP

ron@kobus.us
to me ▾

Thu, Jun 16, 2:08 PM (5 days ago) ☆ ↩ ⋮

Marnie

I was just talking about you guys the other day to an MSP. He was having retention problems so I asked him if he was doing QBRS. Well, guess what the answer was.

By keeping top of mind with my clients, I've seen projects come out of a QBR that I would not have otherwise known about. "I've got this big project... maybe we should talk about updating computers." You become their business partner.

I needed to continue to be in touch. That's what I get with Lifecycle. Retention more than pays back the time and investment in the QBR. It's all about the relationship.

—RON COTSOPOULOS
Kobus Technologies

The Secret

QBRs are a key component to Customer Success. And CS starts before a prospect is a customer.

You might be asking: "Are you saying we do a QBR before a prospect is a client?"

Yes. Yes, we are.

Your "sales presentation" is going to show them what working with you looks like. Because of this, it isn't going to feel like a presentation at all. It is going to feel like a polished QBR.

It is going to be a strategic business consultation, because that is what great MSPs do.

You are going to ask them about their business goals and objectives. You are going to ask how technology supports (or doesn't support) those goals. You are going to ask them what keeps them up at night.

Then you are going to listen. You will take notes. You will clarify, and you will ask how they have tried to solve these problems in the past.

(*The MSP Handbook: Sales Edition* will fill in the gaps here.)

Sample Presentation Meeting

Your prospect thinks they are walking into a typical sales call. They are wrong. When you frame it like the example below, they will immediately understand your MSP's unique value proposition:

> Thanks for taking the time to meet with me again. I have enjoyed getting to know a bit about your business and your team.
>
> Last time we met, you said that you were growing a ton and planning to open a second location, but all of the recent ransomware attacks in the news kept you up at night. Of course, you would really rather be spending those nights at your new beach house. I think we can help with that.
>
> In talking with some of your team, we also heard about frustrations caused by laggy older devices. They also mentioned the big win of a new billing system that gives the accounting department more time to work on those revenue targets. It is always a good sign for a company when employees appreciate the value of new technologies and how they support their work, not steal their jobs.
>
> Let's talk about how we can save your employees more time and get you to that beach house.

At this point, you can dive into some simple reports to show how you are going to move the needle for this company. This report will mirror those used in a QBR.

> *For a full sample QBR report, visit:*
>
> **theMSPhandbook.com**

These reports need to be high level and easy to read. Stoplight reports with red, yellow, and green indicators and risks, along with a view of "Before" and "After" are ideal. If you show them the path to the beach house, they will come along for the ride.

Know the "NO"

 In typical Juan fashion, I learned this the hard way. The company was AOL. The department was Cancellations. Nobody was calling me to say yes.

In my early years I worked in a startup call center for America Online. All I heard was "No" about 200 times a day.

Oftentimes we take "No" at face value. When we hear it once or twice, we chalk it up to something related to the person who delivered the No. But when you pay attention, what you learn is there is a pattern to them. Ironically, there is a "Yes" hidden inside.

Each day I would leave work feeling semi-defeated, rehashing the negativity I had heard. I would think about how I might have said or done something differently to convert them to a YES.

No one likes to hear No when your job requires a Yes. I began to really despise the word. But I wasn't willing to accept defeat.

I decided to change my mindset.

I embraced the "No." I made "No" my friend. I made "No" my greatest ally. In fact, I learned to *love* "No."

As I dug deeper, I found a pattern in the No's.

The first "No" actually meant "I don't understand your value proposition."

The second "No" meant "I don't see how this will solve my problem or work for me."

The third "No" is the one that meant "I can't afford it."

The secret is knowing the "No" that's coming next and embracing it. Once I knew what was coming, and why, it helped me to formulate my talk track and remove the "No."

If you can help your customers understand your actual value, by showing them how your product or service will change their company/life and positively impact them (aka that beach house), you will be able to demonstrate how they can't afford *not* to do business with you. This will comfort them and overcome their fear of uncertainty.

Value Chains—Turning the No to Yes

Below are some critical elements used in unlocking the "Yes!"

Take a good look at this graphic below, and imagine the process, turning that flywheel we mentioned.

Keys to Unlocking the "YES"

Always WIN Mentality: Leave with a Deal, Learn a lesson, Build a Relationship

🗝 What is the outcome the customer wants to achieve?

🗝 What are the financial impacts the customer will achieve with the outcome?

🗝 How will your plan get the customer to the desired outcome?

🗝 What business process are they targeting for change and how will they change?

🗝 What technology solutions will need to be implemented to ensure the outcome?

🗝 Simply illustrate the plan to deliver the business outcomes and clarify benefits.

🗝 Deliver a successful outcome

Read the list above again!

As you consider those keys, what did you notice? Yep—the secret! The QBR process *is* your sales process.

Takeaways

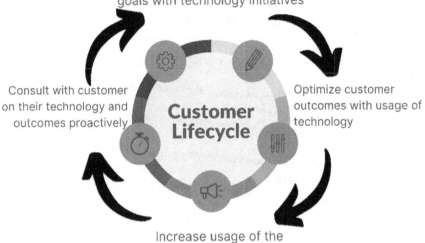

Consult on how to align business goals with technology initiatives

Consult with customer on their technology and outcomes proactively

Customer Lifecycle

Optimize customer outcomes with usage of technology

Increase usage of the technology solution(s)

PART 2
THE WHAT

CHAPTER 3

The 3 Key Value Drivers

"Don't drive customers into the hands of the competitor by not having a diverse offering."

—Juan Fernandez

One of the biggest challenges that we see in managed services is that we often only communicate Features and Benefits. The true driver of sales, however, is Outcomes. Let's illustrate this with an example. We will walk through this step by step to clarify.

Have you ever stopped to think about why diet plans are so popular? Why do we like them? Because they give us a plan... *with Outcomes!*

They demonstrate personal Outcomes that help us set desired goals like: lose weight, reduce cancer risk, manage Diabetes, prevent heart attack/stroke, strengthen bones and teeth, improve mood, improve sleep, and improve memory.

Just like in technology, there are so many plans that could work, but none of them will be effective if we don't first identify the goals of the end-user.

Next, diet plans help people know what data to collect, and what to do with it once they have it.

As MSPs, we must give our clients proper guidance by collecting and analyzing information so we can make technology recommendations, set benchmarking, and offer education and ongoing support that will help them reach the outcomes they identified. Because end-users typically don't know how to ask technical questions (and often can't understand technical explanations), this step is crucial to the achievement of Customer Success.

Diet plans aim to help people achieve their diet goals... *though rarely do they succeed!*

As an MSP, you have the power to do better. You can not only help your clients reach and achieve their desired outcomes, but through QBRs, you can demonstrate value and offer transformation for the years ahead.

 Features—What You See

Let's start with *Features* because this one is easy for most people. In fact, that's why so often product and service descriptions are long on Features but short on explaining Outcomes.

Features are attributes like size, shape, color, function, and process. A diet Feature would include how many calories you can consume, types of foods you can or can't indulge in, and how often you should eat. For services or other intangible offerings, Features are the steps in the process and how it works. For example, that might be the number of meetings included, follow-up support, or bonus elements.

In all cases, people need to know what something will look like—literally or figuratively. Describing the Features of a product or service establishes base expectations and provides context.

Benefits—What You Get Immediately

Benefits are the short-term, future-focused advantages to be gained as a result of the product's or service's features.

What can you do or experience immediately because of how the product is designed and functions?

Typically these are demonstrated with "because" statements that show what a Feature can instantly provide. For example: "Because you committed to your diet for four weeks, you have lost weight."

Benefits offer insight into what makes the product or service unique. They build the case for why the offering would be a better buy than the competition.

The Triple B: Because = Benefits = Build the case

Outcomes—What You Experience Long-term

Outcomes describe the transformations that result from using the product or service. They bring emotion into the mix. That's why they are so powerful.

For example: "Now you are living a healthier lifestyle—living longer and enjoying time with your family more."

Whereas Benefits are about short-term advantages, Outcomes speak to long-term gains. They paint a vision of the future where your customers have resolved their challenges and met their aspirations.

Outcomes are a result of the Benefits, just as Benefits are a result of Features.

The QBR Your Customer Deserves

Let's play a little game of MadLibs™. On a scrap of paper write a response for each of the following (or just write in the book!):

1. Name a complicated medical term_____

2. Name a car part_____

3. Name your favorite technical gadget_____

4. Name a large number_____

5. Name your least favorite trouble ticket_____

Now use your responses to fill in the blanks:

Hello Mr./Mrs. Customer!

It is time for your business review. I am excited to talk to you about your problems with (1)_____and how some (2)_____ and (3)_____ might help. Also we have some ideas on how (4) _____could solve these problems, and of course I want to review all of our tickets around (5)_____. When can we schedule that review?

In that one (hopefully) imaginary conversation, we see the makings of objections MSPs often hear when trying to schedule business reviews.

First, overly technical and/or complicated language makes it sound like Charlie Brown's teacher is delivering the business review. "*Mwamp, mwamp, mwamp-mwamp-mwamp.*"

Second, it comes off like a sales pitch.

Third, it sounds like an autopsy or a historical review. Patch stats. Ticket summaries. Number of spams anti-spammed and viruses anti-virused.

If your customer previously suffered through a business review like this, it probably didn't deliver value. So let's turn that around and talk about how to deliver QBRs that don't suck!

Goals

 People often ask me if there are similarities between my job as a high school math teacher and working in the IT industry. There are more than you think, but if you answer this question, you will see the most obvious similarity.

Think back to your days in high school. What was the most popular question in your math class?

When am I ever going to use this stuff?

Remember Simon Sinek's *Start with Why*? I always believed it was my responsibility to get students to understand *why* we used mathematics, so I could convince them to *do* the mathematics. The same is true in a business review. If your customers believe the *why* (the "outcomes" Juan outlined earlier), then they will buy.

The key here for MSPs to understand is that your *why* is not about specific technologies but rather about serving as a business/IT consultant.

Technology helps businesses do a few things:

- Save time

- Develop efficiencies and consistent business practices

- Become more profitable

- Eliminate human error

- Increase employee retention

- Reduce the need for FTEs
  (full-time equivalents, especially important
  in a tough labor market/economy)

- Be a competitive differentiation

- Optimize the business

Let's look at some ways to communicate with clients and help them understand that your QBRs will be all about them and their business goals.

Hierarchy of Needs

I find that frameworks are a great way to get everybody on the same page quickly. They paint a picture for the client as well. Since we all know that a picture is worth a thousand words, let's paint the picture of how your client can think about technology as part of their business.

Aligning your framework with something familiar adds clarity and strength. I have drawn something like the diagram on the following page on

> *Let your QBR show clients the answer to: "When am I ever going to use this?"*

many business reviews. It is a way to get clients to understand that you need to build a strong foundation together in order for them to achieve their goals.

Maslow's hierarchy focuses on the things every human needs in order to survive. They are ranked based on priority.

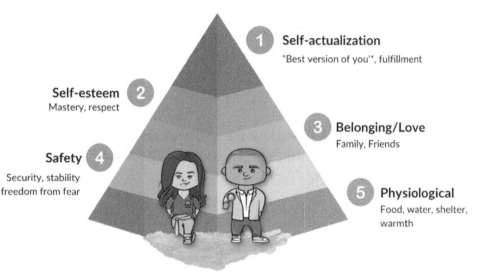

Let's start at the bottom. It is no surprise that food, air, and water come before all other needs. As you move up the pyramid, you see the need for security, belonging and family, the need for respect, and finally becoming the best version of yourself that you can possibly be.

Some mockingly argue that in the current day and age this hierarchy has been changed...

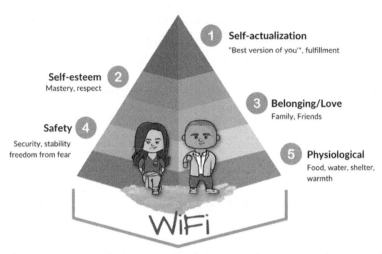

They argue that Wi-Fi is now the most basic need. But jokes aside, this is a good way to get your clients thinking about structuring priorities.

Now you can present the hierarchy of their technology needs.

Priorities start at the bottom. While you and your clients want to talk about Outcomes, if they are stuck with outdated assets that cause downtime, then they are going to struggle. You cannot implement a paradigm-shifting technology that revolutionizes a business if people can't process credit cards to get paid.

Next, their work environment needs to be safe and protected. Their competitive differentiator will make zero impact if ransomware shuts them down for days.

MSPs often tell us they struggle to get clients to understand the importance of asset lifecycle management and best security practices. It is certainly not the most interesting conversation your business partners want to have. This hierarchy, however, shows them that both are critical in order to be able to have the conversations they really want to have with you and their own customers.

If we think about Maslow's hierarchy, who wouldn't rather talk about lifelong aspirations? A business owner wants to talk about their goals and accomplishments for the same reason. Using this hierarchy will help them understand you need to first provide them with a strong foundation to get there.

Cadence

I recently attended a presentation on operational maturity of MSPs. Using data collected from thousands of MSPs, there was a conversation about differentiation and valuation.

The most profitable MSPs could be identified by answering the following two questions:

1. How much of their revenue is based on Monthly Recurring Revenue (MRR)?

2. What percent of their clients get true Quarterly Business Reviews?

The closer the second question's answer was to 100%, the more likely the answer to the first question would be higher. This is because having business reviews with clients quarterly drives the right conversations and the right sentiment around using technology as a business strategy. It helps to ensure a focus on alignment to your stack.

Before you toss the book on the floor in exasperation (especially if you are reading the kindle version!), know that this will be a work in progress. No one is eating the elephant in one bite. Let's talk about a plan for moving toward true quarterly business reviews. And... let's keep in mind that they won't all look the same. (This should be a comfort to you.)

Think about where you are presently on the spectrum of business review maturity.

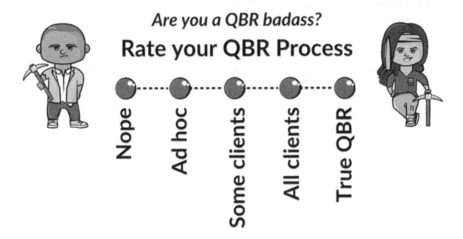

If you are doing true QBRs, congratulate yourself and your team. You are a QBR badass and can skip to Chapter 4 to learn about QBR best practices. It is an iterative process so there is always room to grow and improve.

Otherwise, let's dig in. First, we need to establish a segment and cadence for each client. (Note: If you have read *Literally: The Book on Customer Success for MSPs*, this will be a quick refresher.)

> *If you haven't already downloaded the bonuses*
> *associated with this book, head to:*
>
> **theMSPhandbook.com**

Let's dive in to our segmentation chart:

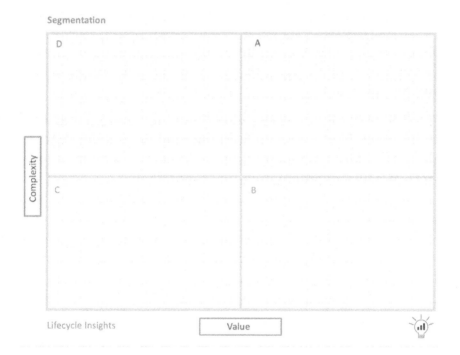

As you look at this workbook page, I want you to think about just a few of your clients.

First, let's consider a value metric of Monthly Recurring Revenue (MRR). Next, think about an effort metric.

If a client is in a high compliance business, your work with them around security could be high-touch. Or you may have clients with multiple locations. Visualize those clients you feel require the most effort. I'm sure you know who they are.

Place the name of a client that has low MRR value and high effort score in the top left quadrant, and one that has high MRR value and high effort score in the top right quadrant.

Now think of your favorite client. Are they high-value/low-effort? If not, pick one that is. They're not very needy. They pay well and are likely your most profitable clients.

Place the name of this client in the bottom right quadrant.

Now you might also have some clients that don't require much effort but also don't pay you much money. Put them in the lower left quadrant.

The amount of touch each quadrant requires coordinates with the chart below. Both top quadrants are high-touch, the bottom right would be mid-touch, and the lower left is tech-touch clients (yes, lots of automation for these folks).

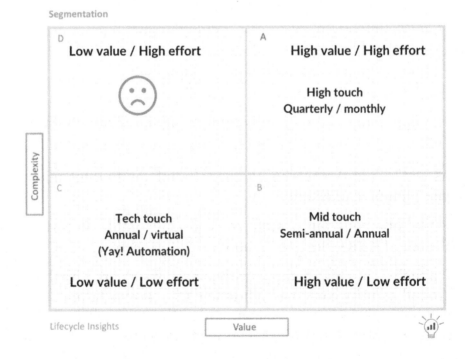

For each quadrant, we need to establish a cadence of how often they need a business review. True QBR clients have reviews quarterly, or early on it might even be monthly.

For the bottom right quadrant (mid-touch clients who offer high MRR value for low effort), how often do you want to meet with them? Are they semi-annual?

For those in the lower left quadrant (tech-touch clients with low MRR value and low effort), could you do an annual face-to-face business review? Could this be conducted virtually? The biggest question for this group is how to stay top of mind even though it would not be profitable for you to regularly meet face-to-face.

This is where marketing content can provide a lot of value. Having a newsletter to remind current clients of best practices can serve as touch points that keep your business and offerings front and center. For example, send friendly reminders like "It's cybersecurity awareness month. That's why we... (fill in the blank)."

Remember if you are not communicating with your clients, somebody else could be. Even if they are not getting face-to-face meetings with you, you need to set a cadence for how to communicate. Just because you aren't planning to do quarterly business reviews does not mean that your clients don't need to be reminded of the value you deliver. Use the power of your marketing/CRM platform to deliver targeted content around what your clients need to hear.

Now, we haven't talked about the top left quadrant yet, though I suspect—since we've talked about all of the clients we actually like working with and who are profitable—we know who is left over to land in this quadrant. They are high-effort/low-value clients. Think of a couple of examples from your own client base.

You have some decisions to make. You can move these clients to the right by renegotiating and having them pay a higher

MRR. Or you can find ways to make them decrease the effort required to serve them. Perhaps there are things you can automate for them? Are there outstanding technical issues that have been causing too many support requests? Can you prioritize these projects and move the client to the tech-touch quadrant? Or maybe they are just not a good fit for your company...

> Nerd alert: If you have read *The Pumpkin Plan* by Mike Michalowicz, these clients are the pumpkins you pluck.

Getting Your Customers to the Table

Now that we have defined how we are going to segment our client base for business reviews and communications, we should talk about how we are going to get our customers to the table.

The first step should have been handled in presales. We talked about showing them what working with you will be like. Now that they are looking forward to strategic conversations, you make that a part of your contract. (NOTE: The worst place you will ever find yourself is in court having to defend your actions on delivery of quarterly business reviews that you stated in your contract.)

> *Voice of an MSP*
>
> *Recently, on a weekly workshop with our partners, Matt Clarin told us how he leveled up his practices around business reviews. His company used to want 90 days to dig in and explore the network before their first official review with recommendations.*
>
> "We were really missing the boat—and an opportunity—by waiting 90 days. We have found that if we start by meeting right after onboarding we can: establish how we have already moved the needle for them; set the expectation right out of the gate that we would be having regular strategic meetings; avoid misunderstandings about what was truly a priority for the client, as the longer you wait to get in touch, the more they believe you

should have accomplished; and most importantly, take the opportunity to build the relationship. By talking about their goals, we no longer had to guess at how to prioritize recommendations for them."

—MATT CLARIN
President, Hungerford Technologies

Now that we have some ideas about getting clients to the table, let's talk about the agenda for your QBR and what you will be discussing.

Here's your opportunity to learn from my mistakes. Have a plan for them, or they will have a plan for you.

We had a very high-value client—the kind who always reminded us they were high-value. We very much hoped to grow the relationship. With a change of leadership on our end, we knew we should establish regular communication. I invited their execs and our execs to a conversation. I looked at which services they currently used as well as upsell opportunities. Included in the agenda, I wrote the word "tickets" and got ready for the day.

The presentation began...

Before I could even start, the project manager had gotten into the ear of the executives. We started a full-on autopsy of previous and current tickets. What I had envisioned as a strategic conversation around best practices and next steps turned into a firing line. I had walked in hoping for strategy but left with a tactical beat-down.

Lesson learned. The next time I scheduled a review with them, I sent out a common agenda two weeks in advance. I included the high-level questions I knew they wanted to engage in and asked if they had any items they would like to address. If they mentioned a particular ticket or escalation, I would hop on a call with our support team to make sure things were happening, then call the client to let them know the issue was too important to wait two weeks to discuss. They immediately felt valued and important.

When you can solve customer satisfaction issues before you get to the business review, it puts them in a happy place and sets the table for strategy instead.

Another advantage of sending an agenda in advance is putting the client in the right frame of mind for a strategic conversation. We have talked to thousands of MSPs about what questions they ask of their business partners to ensure they deliver value at a QBR. The true key to a business review is that it is about business and how technology supports it—not strictly about technology. (Remember "Outcomes" not "Features"?)

How can you forecast this concept through an agenda? Let's see what our partners say.

The Components of a QBR

The Agenda

Establishing regular questions about your customer's business goals and changes in their industry is an ideal way to get the conversation started. Here are a few:

- How is your business changing over the next 12–18 months?

- Are you planning an expansion or adding new locations?

- Are you downsizing or closing locations?

- Are you hiring? Do you plan any other major staffing changes in the upcoming months?

- What is changing in the industry? Commoditization? Growth? New technologies?

- What are three things you wish technology could do for you?

We recently held a workshop featuring a panel of experienced MSP owners who shared best practices around how to drive strategic conversation and business reviews.

Tricia King, Senior Consultant/vCIO for Vertikal6, shared how they discover their clients' organizational goals and then work to align their technology with those goals.

Here is a snapshot from her agenda:

Strategic Goal	Aligned Technology Goal	Status
Continue to grow through acquisition	Develop a playbook for gathering information required for technology and service integration.	
	Define a technology and security standard for new acquisitions to determine a clearer path to necessary infrastructure changes.	Not started
Revitalize the organization with a new brand.	Plan for underlying technology changes to email, Active Directory, internal applications, and website.	Not started

When business owners realize they're coming to a *strategic* business review, they start contemplating new strategies around:

- How to optimize their current processes

- How to make their teams more efficient

- How to lighten the load on stressed staff

They will be sure to schedule that next business review before you leave the meeting. That's the power of having an agenda.

QBR Prep for a Strategic Meeting

Beyond the agenda, what do you prepare for the meeting?

We have seen a lot of different Standard Operating Procedures (SOPs) around how MSPs prepare for a business review. That said, one thing they have in common is that they all focus on efficiency and accuracy of what will be presented.

For insights on a successful QBR process,
our friends over at Team ELBO have donated a template.
It can be found here:

theMSPhandbook.com

Included in ELBO's doc is an outline of the data they collect.

Thanks,
Team ELBO!

The Data

The key here is to collect data that will inform your team of risks, opportunities, and any potential inefficiencies that the customer will be able to see within the business.

The ideal state is to be able to automate as much of this reporting as possible. The obvious data collection lies around those inventories that are required by cybersecurity liability insurance companies and many of the security frameworks (NIST, CIS, CMMC and other 3-4 letter acronyms):

- *Asset lifecycle management reporting.* This includes data around warranty and end of life status.

- *User reporting.* At a minimum this should include reconciliation of users that are in your existing PSA and Microsoft or other licensing. There is an increased need for reporting around inactive licenses as well as the security on those licenses (such as whether MFA is enabled).

- *Scans of the environment and network.* Shadow IT is included here. NOTE: These reports are not delivered at a business review but instead curated in responses within the assessment (see Chapter 4).

- *Metrics and other data.* Present trend data in support of KPIs that drive business outcomes. The conversation around tickets, patching, antivirus, and backups should only be used in cases where relevant to outcomes.

While our industry says that many of those metrics are "table stakes," recognize that while they are important, they are just a baseline expectation and should not be part of a strategic conversation.

The Assessment

The meat of the conversation in a business review will be prioritizing what you learned as you ran a risk assessment for your client. Numerous templates and assessments can be used to deliver the conversation. Some are based around categories like hardware, software, security, or compliance.

SUMMARY

The overall summary report provides an overall score for each of the categories designed to show the overall health and compliance of your IT systems. Scores are weighted based on their respective importance to keeping your business in optimal range.

Summary Report for: Creative Designs
Date Prepared: 2022-06-10
Assessment Template: Lifecycle DFLT Assessment

Category	Description	Score
Hardware	Review different components related to client's infrastructure.	67
Business Applications / Software	Software Applications for Operating and Protecting the Business	100
Policy & Procedure	Does the company have the necessary Policies & Procedures in place to provide appropriate protections?	100
Security	Review critical areas of security in place for the client.	75
Continuity	Business Continuity and BDR	83
Regulatory Compliance	Identify and Score Client Compliance Obligations	50
Overall Score		88

The point of the assessment, however, is to determine opportunities within the organization. Use this time to quantify the outcomes you plan to deliver.

Assessments deliver the vision of what you can accomplish for your clients. At every QBR, you should present trend data on the same assessment categories to prove you are achieving those outcomes.

Assessment types we have seen include:

- Leveled security framework assessments like CMMC
- Standards assessments
- Customer health
- Policy and procedures

There are three levels:

- Being in practice
- Having a practice
- Delivering best practices

Quality assessments take time to build. But it is easy to get writer's block if you wait for an assessment to be perfect right out of the gate. Do not let perfect be the enemy of good. This is an iterative process and you must start somewhere or you will never get anywhere.

Consider your standards and best practices. If you're looking for a place to start, here is a guide:

Stack Builder

	Solution	Product	Vendor
1	Firewall		
2	Switches		
3	Wireless		

4	Intrusion Detection and Prevention		
5	Email Hosting		
6	Email Encryption		
7	Email Archiving		
8	Email Protection/Filtering		
9	Email Signature Management		
10	DNS Content Filtering		
11	Cloud Filter Services (SharePoint/Anchor...)		
12	Cloud Services Backup (MS365/Google)		
13	Antivirus (Traditional)		
14	Antimalware (NextGen)		
15	Cybersecurity (Managed SOC)		
16	Zero Trust		
17	Privileged Access Management (PAM)		
18	Workstation/Server Encryption		
19	Backup & Disaster Recovery		
20	Endpoint/Workstation Backup		
21	Data Loss Prevention (DLP)		
22	Mobile Device Encryption		
23	Cloud Directory Services		
24	VPN/Remote Access		
25	Multi-factor Authentication		
26	Password Manager		
27	Secure Scan/Fax		
28	SIEM/Event Log Monitoring		

29	Third Party Audit/Pen Testing		
30	Dark Web Monitoring		
31	Social Engineering/Phishing		
32	Employee Cyber Training		
33	VOIP		
34	Print Management		
35	Website Hosting/Management		
36	Vendor Risk Management		
37	Internet Service Provider		
38	Redundant internet		

Within a chart like this, you can document your standards and best practices in order to develop an assessment aligned to your services. You may find, however, that some standard assessments are already closely aligned to the services you offer and may only need to be tweaked based on your specific technology stack.

A copy of the
Lifecycle Insights Default Assessment
is available at:

theMSPhandbook.com

Once you have a solid draft of your assessment template, you will want to fill it out for a specific client.

Score the client on how they match up to your best practices. Are they at risk? Are there areas that need attention? Maybe there's an acceptable risk? Hopefully there are quite a number of satisfactory responses.

The key in preparing the risk assessment is to identify business risks that can be remediated through technologies or best practices like stronger policies and procedures around security.

With each item in the assessment, understand what status quo looks like for this client. Then determine what remediation can be done. By looking at technology needs in this light it will lead to a better presentation to the CEO, who is more concerned about eliminating risk than about widgets or gadgets.

Components of a completed assessment should:

1. *Deliver impact.* Right out of the gate the stoplight scoring makes it clear to the business owner what is a threat (red) and what is in good shape (green). Include comments why this is a concern as well as your remediation plan to connect the dots for non-technical CEOs.

2. *Deliver consistency.* Internally, it is important to also document scoring instructions and how your company will recommend remediation steps based on a poor score. This ensures consistency across account managers or vCIOs. It also ensures that industry knowledge the CEO or account owner has will not leave the company if they do.

3. *Save time.* Having this documentation in place also allows for multiple team members to work within an assessment in a consistent fashion. We often see interns or tier-one techs responding based on well written documentation and high-level engineers being able to quickly jump in and respond to the few questions that only they can answer.

As with any assessment, if you merely collect data and don't review it to identify required actions, then you never should have wasted the time collecting it in the first place. (Yes, we can wait while you jot a note to review which of your systems are collecting data that never get used.)

The Recommendations

Once you have the assessment complete, it's time to show your true value as an MSP. This is where your expertise and knowledge allows you to prioritize the "at-risk" and "needs-attention" items and build recommendations on how to resolve those business concerns. Connecting the dots for your clients is the most powerful way you can align customers to best practices while increasing supportability, scalability, and security.

The critical element of recommendations is tying together the risk to the business with the resolution. When a business owner understands the need for remediation (The Why), they will accept the cost (The What).

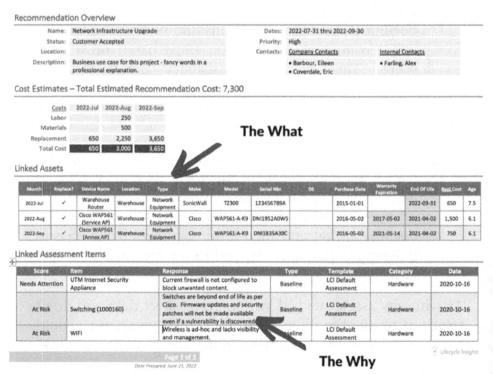

Once those recommendations are built, it is now time to review the budget. For many small businesses this is their favorite part of the review.

Yep, hard to believe, but it is true... business owners like to be presented with a budget!

You might be thinking:

At no point has any business owner *ever* been excited for me to present a quote for new projects.

Correct! But presenting a quote is not the same thing as offering a budget. That difference is crucial.

The Budget

Think back to Juan's lesson around "Knowing the No." It gives you the power to turn budget opportunities into a Yes! When conversations with your client only culminate in unexpected expenses for the business owner, that person is less likely to want to meet with you in the future. They will equate meeting with you to mean spending money they don't want to spend.

Remember, during the QBR, you are not making a sales call. You are engaging in a strategic conversation. Delivering a budget forecast to your client secures your seat at the table as a trusted partner for the future.

When doing strategic budgeting, recognize that every dollar spent by your client needs to translate into a dollar earned for your client's business. As a strategic partner, one of the most impactful things you can do is to deliver a comprehensive, annual technology budget. This should include expenses for your services, proposed projects, and third-party costs associated with technology. This budget should illustrate how you are able to empower their business to be even more successful.

This gives your clients permission to say yes to your next meeting because they know you won't blindside them. They will say yes to budgeting for their needs because they will know, in advance, what those needs really are.

Done well, clients may even say yes to your suggestion to simply send a purchase order when it's time for new asset purchases because they trust the relationship and your plan.

> *When doing strategic budgeting, recognize that every dollar spent by your client needs to translate into a dollar earned for your client's business.*

If you have never delivered a budget at a business review before, you might be wondering why you would want to remind them how much they're going to pay you. *"I could just bring additional project quotes and try to sell them on those."* But that would be missing the point of the budget.

The power of a strategic conversation comes from delivering a total technology budget. This includes delivery of all existing services. It also includes recommendations to solve the pains found in the risk assessment.

Imagine adding third-party contracts around things such as:

- Line of business applications
- Process software such as ERP or CRM platforms
- Printer copiers
- Phone providers
- ISP providers

Many small businesses would consider these items as technology expenses but they have never truly built a full technology budget. Outlining short-term expenditures as well as a long-term roadmap is a powerful tool you can deliver.

Chris Wiser, an MSP coach, says:

"Budgets don't get cut... expenses do."

If you merely speak about your services, the immediate reaction is to attempt to reduce the cost of those services. But if you are the one bringing a budget to the table, you get to establish a roadmap for your partners.

Not only does this bring value to your clients, but it brings value to you as well. We often see MSPs who have delivered budgets to their clients become the focal point of the budgeting conversation.

Their clients happily provide information around additional technology costs, for example a high-dollar Salesforce expense. Knowing when the $30,000 Salesforce bill is due helps the MSP avoid a conversation around replacing two servers in the same month knowing that funds are tight.

When you have insights into services your clients are paying for outside of your agreement, you may find things you could be providing for them instead. For example, they may have a phone provider that is not included in your current service. If you know when that contract is expiring, you can ask if they would like to review your preferred service instead.

Voice of an MSP

"We explained to a prospect that we would deliver a full budget projection and technology roadmap for them during our presales conversation. We asked if they could provide recent billing contracts to assist us. In doing so, we discovered they were actually using 17 different phone services.

We were able to eliminate these 17 phone bills and save them $3,000 a month while moving them to a managed service contract with us that included a large project for onboarding with a recurring revenue of $4,000 a month. If we hadn't asked for information to deliver that budget, we would never have had such an easy conversation for the sale. The new client was over the moon about the savings and realized the value we brought to the table."

—WILLIAM POTE
CEO, eTop Technology

William will be the first to admit that delivering budget proposals to prospects (rather than only to clients) creates much more up-front work. Before offering this level of presales service you should ensure the prospect will be a good-fit customer for your MSP.

Two kinds of budgets can be presented: short-term (6–12 months) and long-term (3–5 years). The former should delineate asset replacement and other expenses. The latter forecasts larger expenses to eliminate future surprise, giving them permission to say "yes" when the time is right.

April-June 2022

Category	Quantity	Budget Cost
Workstation ➕	1	79
Network Equipment ➖	3	3,050

Asset	User	Make/Vendor	Model Number	Serial Number	Age	EOL	Repl Cost	Wty Renewal Cost	Comments
Cisco SF 200 Switch		Cisco	SF200-24	9466309827157	6.2	2022-04-02	2,000	0	
Wireless Access Point Lewes		Cisco	AP541N-A-K9	9466309827493	6.2	2022-04-02	300	0	
New Dallas Wireless Setup - Cisco WAP561 (Cluster config)		Cisco	Cisco WAP561		6.1	2022-05-02	750	0	

Software ➕	1	900
Contracts/Subscriptions ➕	1	500
Recommendations ➕	1	2,000
Subtotal for April-June 2022:	7	6,529

Budget Forecast for Creative Designs

Current Reporting Options: ⚙ ▾   Warranty Renewal Costs: On | Suppress Zero Rows: On | Overdue: On | Not Scheduled: On | Group by Year- Showing 6 Year/s | Categories:
Network Equipment, Printer, Server, Software, Virtual Server, Workstation

DETAIL VIEW   SPREADSHEET VIEW

Component Expand All	Overdue	Not Scheduled	2022	2023	2024	2025	2026
Server ➕	0	0	1	0	0	0	0
Virtual Server ➕	3,000	0	0	0	0	0	0
Workstation ➕	13,737	0	79	6,151	15,600	0	0
Network Equipment ➕	9,798	0	4,175	750	1,148	2,150	0
Software ➕	0	0	900	400	0	0	950
Printer ➕	0	0	0	5,000	0	0	0
Totals	26,535	0	5,155	12,301	16,748	2,150	950

Budget components include:

- Expiring assets
- Ongoing contracts and subscriptions
    - Those provided by your MSP
    - 3rd-party contracts
- Recommendation and remediation costs

Some MSPs deliver two rounds of budgets: one after they've established the status quo, and a second where they include prioritized recommendations. The beauty of using a platform or tool to deliver a budget during your QBR is the ease to adjust it on the fly as clients accept and approve or deny projects.

Voice of an MSP, continued

William Pote of eTop Technologies signed up for a 30-day free trial of Lifecycle Insights' platform in November 2019. The following week he had two end-of-year QBRs, so over the weekend he prepared asset lifecycle management reports. Between just those two QBRs, he sold $100,000 worth of refresh projects.

"Business owners don't like to see red. I showed them the report and told them to 'Get the red out.' They did."

Next he started assessments, identifying risk. Red still drove the conversation. There were two outcomes. His best clients became even more profitable, increasingly aligned to his stack of services, making them easier to support, secure, and scale. It also helped him weed out the bad clients. He made more money from fewer clients.

That leads us into the next conversation. As you begin to plan delivery of your business reviews, it is fair to ask: "How long should a QBR be?"

Delivery

Mark Twain once wrote, "I apologize for the long letter. If I had more time I would've written you a short one." This applies directly to how long your QBR should last. If it is your first time, it may be 90 minutes to 2 hours, but as you iterate your process and the relationship grows, a QBR can be delivered inside an hour.

This isn't the first time, nor will it be the last time we mention iteration. In Chapter 4 we will walk you through the process maturity model, providing tactical steps to improve your business review regardless of where you are starting.

For now, focus on how to deliver your next QBR based on what you've been learning here.

- How can you present risk without being a gross sales person?

- How can you explain risk without accepting liability?

It should be no surprise that communication is critical. Keep in mind that the business owner you are speaking to will be an expert in their business—but not an expert in technology. They need to hear the risks in language they can understand, presented in simple graphs and summary data using red, yellow, and green indicators.

This is how you avoid being salesy. People understand data without you needing to use "FUD" tactics: triggering fear, uncertainty, and doubt.

Presenting risk in this manner simplifies the conversation so you won't confuse your client along the way (because a confused mind says No).

The next step is aligning risk to your recommendations. Not only will you have identified their risk, but you will have outlined a remediation plan to address it for them.

As for the question of liability, use this language:

> *"How would you like to address the risk we have uncovered in your environment today?"*

Read that suggested wording again and think about the tone it portrays. You as technology consultants have identified their risk. You have outlined possible remediation strategies. It is *their risk* and you are simply asking how they would like to address it.

If you're struggling to ask clients about budget, try this language:

"In working with other clients
similar to your business
in size, vertical and location,
we have been able to solve
and address problems
like these for about $2000 to $3000 a month.
How does that sound?"

Asking the question this way will get you a couple possible responses.

- "Oh, $2000? I wasn't planning on paying more than $1500."

    o Budget acquired.

- "Yeah, that sounds about right. I think we can do that."

    o Now you know what you need to present when you come back with your budget proposal.

- "That's all?"

    o Next time up your prices.

Juan's always-win mentality:

- You build a relationship...
- You learn a lesson...
- Or you win a deal

In this case, if the customer is not interested in your price, you have both learned a lesson and built a relationship.

Approaching the conversation about risk and mitigation this way accomplishes several things. It communicates that the business has a problem or risk that you can solve. That solution has a cost... and it will be an ongoing expense to keep their business stable, secure, and scaling. You are not offering line-item expenses or offering an à la carte menu from which they can pick and choose. Not only this, you will have prompted them to share the budget number you were looking for.

Above and beyond all these things, you will have had a strategic conversation about their business. As you close the meeting, there are two must-dos.

1. Summarize their business goals.

2. Summarize the action items you have agreed upon to help them reach those goals. (This should include their action items and yours so everyone understands who is accountable.)

The Executive Summary

The general flow of your QBR should have three parts. Why? Because people remember the first and last things they hear.

Therefore, start the business review from the agenda you sent ahead of time, discussing their business goals and high-level questions so they begin to think about new initiatives and supporting their objectives.

Next, deliver the meat of the presentation, then end with an Executive Summary—an easy to consume summary of takeaways so they can leave the room with enthusiasm and excitement about the work to be done. This reminds them how you are helping them improve their business.

This Executive Summary also makes asking the next question easy:

"Have I delivered value in this meeting?"

If they say no, you need to first address that.

If they say yes, now you have a follow-up question.

*"Do you know other businesses
that could benefit from
the same type of conversation?"*

Yep! This is how you ask for the referral.

> PRO TIP: Here are other questions you can ask before leaving
> the table:
>
> 1. "What was something positive about this meeting?"
>
> 2. "What was something you would change?"
>
> 3. "What would you like to make sure we address next time?"
>
> 4. "When should we schedule our next meeting?"

In sales acronyms, that last question points to the strategy called BAMFAM—Book A Meeting From A Meeting. It doesn't sound salesy when your customer is totally on board and it's their idea to schedule the next meeting.

To set the proper cadence, find out what works best for the customer, but here is one suggestion. In the first 90 days, it can be an expectation to meet monthly around these objectives: 30 days for onboarding, 30 for implementation, and 30 for Customer Success and strategic planning. At that point, you will have a better understanding of how your customer feels about cadence.

> PRO TIP: You can never meet too much when it comes to strategic conversations. It is all about building trust and deepening the relationship. Offer two cadence options that work for you and see what works for them.

In a down economy, it is critical to stop selling and start helping. Guess where this happens: in a QBR.

But what if you delivered a bad QBR in the past and your clients don't want to meet? What are some strategies you can do to recover?

If a client thinks you're just there to sell or talk tech, you can understand why they might be hesitant. If that is what happened previously, then you must show them what will be different about your next meeting.

Be honest. Call them and say:

> "I know in previous meetings we have done sales presentations or talked about gadgets and widgets that were not your top priority. We have been doing research in your industry about how to conduct strategic meetings to look at your business goals instead. Every CEO I have talked to has a wish list of what they hope technology can do for them. We would love to hear your needs and business goals to see if there are ways we can help you address them more efficiently or economically."

Remember to stop delivering patch stats, exhausting ticket reviews, and info about spam filtering and how many viruses you anti-virused for the client. Your goal is to deliver value above and beyond a minimal contractual commitment.

Follow-up

Part of your QBR should be a follow-up of how you have moved the needle for your client. In your pre-sales meeting with prospects, you outlined all the ways your offerings could provide not just features and benefits, but also outcomes for their business. Here is the time when you show them where they stood then vs. where they stand now.

You also need to clearly follow up your own action items resulting from the business review, as stated within your Executive Summary.

You need a process for *relentless* follow-up from your QBR. Each action item from a recommendation needs to be documented. Tickets need to be made. Promises need to be kept. Remember our initial discussion about how Customer

Success is key to growing your business? Your follow-up here is a large part of that!

Takeaways

The QBR Checklist

- Agenda
- Customer ROI statements (focus on their goals!)
- Risk assessment
- Recommendations/Technology business goal alignment
- Technology budgets
  - Short-term
  - Long-term
- Supporting inventories
  - Asset reports
  - User and phishing reports
  - Contracts
- Executive Summary (again, focus on their outcomes!)
- Take-away action items and a plan for follow-up

PART 3
THE HOW

CHAPTER 4

Start Somewhere. Start Now.

 At industry events and conferences, I love to ask MSPs what they think about business reviews. So often the answer is: "I know we should do them," or "I know we can do them better." Frequently they go on to answer that their coach or peer group says they *must* do them. But then they confess that they don't know how.

Well, QBRs are like the weather. Everybody talks about them, but nobody has done anything about them... *until now!*

First, you have to defeat the blank page syndrome that can stand in the way of all the success you can have on the other side of your first, or next, QBR.

One of my coaching clients, Scott, advised newcomers: "Just go run the default assessment. Do it now. Running anything once will help you tweak and make it better. And running it a second time will help you tweak it even more."

What Scott suggests can be summarized...

Start somewhere. Start now.

If you aren't talking to your clients, your competitors will be. That should be reason enough to get moving on a QBR. But there can be so much stress over creating the *perfect QBR*. Take heart. The only thing better than a perfect QBR is a QBR that's DONE.

If you find yourself battling analysis paralysis about starting QBRs, try thinking of it in lowercase instead of boldface in all caps.

qbr

It's just three little letters, but they can lead to a breakthrough for your MSP and your life. Start anywhere. Start now.

Then iterate.

Process Maturity Model

I suspect you already have a list of ideas from this book about how you would like to implement or improve QBRs in your MSP. Heck, you might even have ten new ideas you want to incorporate. The trick is do so without getting overwhelmed along the way.

Just like any business practice, establishing a solid QBR program requires iteration and continual improvement. Look at where you are now and where you want to be. Each component of a QBR can be examined individually and improved upon... moving from *undefined*, to *manual*, to *digital*, to *automated*, and finally to *transformational*.

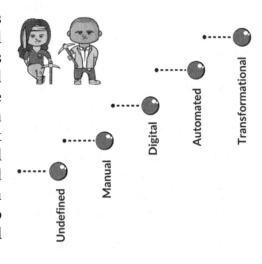

Many times, as folks start a new practice or process—or even a new business—they tackle the steps and actions in an *undefined* fashion. When you instead begin repeating processes, you can define a better way to work.

That next phase, however, is still done in a *manual* fashion. Here you document the steps you are taking (what will one day become your "process") in a spreadsheet. But don't let that spreadsheet stop you from making the next leap. *Automation* is where you can really make an impact. When the data can drive insights for you and your clients, the real *transformation* can occur.

What does our process maturity model look like for a business review?

Let's begin with a single component of the QBR: asset lifecycle management. What does *undefined* look like? Well, when you first started out, you probably weren't tracking warranty status or end-of-life dates for assets. Likely you only reviewed them inside an RMM when an asset started acting up.

Most IT companies quickly move to at least a *manual* process of documenting assets alongside their expiration dates. The obvious place to do this is in a spreadsheet, so now we are already up to the *digital* step.

With pivot tables and conditional formatting, you could start gaining insights into actions you need to take. This still requires updating the spreadsheet continually... which usually gets bumped to the bottom of the to-do list, and promptly falls off.

In comes the power of *automation*. It is possible to move the asset lifecycle tracking into a platform that automatically performs warranty look-ups, identifies purchase dates, and applies asset type policies to trigger when at or approaching end of life. No manual interaction is needed. The data is always up-to-date, with red, yellow, and green lifecycle data delivered straight to an inbox—yours and your client's—automating the entire process... so you can simply take action.

That is where *transformation* comes into play. W. Edwards Deming said, "You can expect what you inspect." When this information is readily available and delivered to clients, their expectation becomes that asset lifecycle management is important. It instantly helps you avoid battles that involve assets which are well beyond their end of life, creating more tickets and anxiety for you and your clients.

In this way, the process maturity model not only saves you time through automation, but it also transforms the way you do business and approach strategic conversations.

If you are brand new to such discussions, ask yourself:

*"How many hours per client per quarter
do I spend managing this conversation?"*

If you are not new to this process, here are some other thoughts on how to iterate where you are:

- How do you set the expectation with your clients that asset lifecycle management is important?

- How are you presently delivering this information to your clients?

- Is this conversation aligned to a business goal?

Voice of an MSP

"Being able to quickly put everything together with Lifecycle Insights made a huge difference—especially during end-of-the-year time crunch. We imported data for a client without manually touching any of it since we weren't planning to present to them for a month. The client came on Dec. 13 and said they needed to spend "an unknown amount of money" in the next two weeks. We worked together for about two hours to increase the data quality, then I was able to provide them with budget forecasts right there on the spot for their own internal review, and let them know we would put together specific recommendations within 48 hours. The next day, we met with the COO and listened to her concerns. They wanted quotes for everything. The following day we supplied those quotes, reviewed it all with them... and within a few days they bought EVERYTHING!"

—MATT ELLIOTT

Sr. Solution Architect, LNS Solutions

Having these conversations at the beginning of your relationship with clients lets you establish the value of asset lifecycle management, security, and scalability. It will also give insights into ways you can work together in the future.

When they realize that technology can help improve their business, you will be treated more like a business consultant than a technology provider.

For Matt Elliott and LNS Solutions, what began as an asset lifecycle management conversation got folded into the managed services agreement. Because his MSP established its ability to quickly and easily provide customers with data to ensure their assets were always up to date, they were able to just send over a quote based on the budget they had presented in earlier QBRs, allowing for a much more scalable, supportable, and strategic relationship.

Scalable Process

So how do you create a process that scales, especially with an eye toward automation? Interestingly enough it is not by starting with automation. It is instead by first defining what the process is.

In the world of QBRs, we are willing to bet you already have some elements that you've cobbled together, even if they're not organized into an official "business review process." Think about the data collection you did during prospecting appointments or onboarding calls. You asked questions, collected data, and hopefully made recommendations.

Now we need to level that up so it becomes repeatable. Once it is repeatable, you can automate it... and once you can automate it, then you're set for exponential growth and success.

If you talk to 100 MSPs, you will learn 100 different ways to deliver managed services and business reviews. As you're looking to scale, let's focus on those elements that get continually repeated. This is where data collection really comes into play.

Remember all the cybersecurity liability insurance companies that require you to do inventories? They require you to run scans. They require you to identify and mitigate risk.

If you are doing any of these repetitive processes manually, your QBR/vCIO platform should make this easy for you to benefit from automating:

- Warranty lookups
- Asset lifecycle management
- User reporting and reconciliation
- Budget forecasting
- Technology roadmapping

Your QBR/vCIO platform should integrate with your PSA and automate each of those reports. The platform should focus on data quality to help ensure accurate and fast reporting. It should also integrate with Microsoft 365 and phishing training platform, and have the power to deliver always up-to-date budget forecasts.

The next step in scaling your transformation is through the risk assessment itself. Begin by listing those questions around your best practices and standards that help to define your MSP and outline risk for your clients.

> *For a starter set of questions,*
> *download the default assessment at:*
>
> **theMSPhandbook.com**
>
> *Revise and make these questions your own.*

Keep in mind that you will continue to iterate. As you can add new items and services, your assessment will change. Make sure your process and any platform you use is flexible enough to support those changes.

Threat actors don't rest on their laurels. Neither can you. Once you have an initial assessment, go run it on your own business. In doing so, document the process. Note the scoring instructions for each item and remediation tips for how your MSP can mitigate risk.

> *Threat actors*
> *don't rest on*
> *their laurels.*
> *Neither can you.*

Having these items documented will allow you to scale the process by handing over work to a tier-one tech (or TAM, or intern, depending on the work required). This frees up the vCIO or owner to focus on more technical and strategic objectives to align to clients' business goals. For example, if expanding services to a new location is a business goal you regularly address, then create a template that outlines the tasks and technology recommendations you provide to support that.

Another way to scale this process is to create an inventory of templates for typical business goals, along with strategic plans to address those goals.

While you will be able to generate assessments using automation, the scoring of them should not be automated. Why? If it could, then MSPs would become complete commodities. While you can and absolutely should run periodic scans to help inform yourself about how to score the assessment, the recommendations you will make should be based on your personal experience and expertise. Using information gathered about your client's business, only you can prioritize next steps and risk mitigation while maximizing and optimizing their technology environment.

PRO TIP: Do not let your strength in technology become a weakness. Bright, shiny objects are fun, but according to that Gartner study we mentioned earlier, 15% of your engagement with your client needs to have the human element. *You* are that human element. Put processes and automation in place to support your work, but know that personally presenting this strategic information is where you will shine.

Measuring Success

We are often asked how MSPs can measure success from QBRs. Like every other part of the process, begin with the end in mind. You cannot assume you already know all the things you will eventually want to measure success, but right out of the gate, you will know whether or not the QBR felt good.

Ask yourself: "Did it deliver value?" When you can answer, "Yes," you'll know you're on the right track.

As mentioned earlier, we've seen initial QBRs take 90 minutes to 2 hours. The more strategic and goal-focused your QBR becomes, the less time it will require. Most MSPs aim to deliver the presentation in 60–90 minutes. But a better word than *presentation* would be *conversation.*

The true measure of success is when your clients want to come back to the next QBR because you've delivered so much value.

This success will also manifest financially, as your business reviews deliver new project revenue, recurring revenue, and more profitable clients who are aligned to your stack and best practices. This alignment metric will eventually become one you can examine to determine future success.

Takeaways

Focus on business goals supported by technology initiatives. If you are looking for ways to approach this, steal some of these:

- Increase innovation
- Lower overall human capital cost
- Decrease overall expenses
- Increase customer adoption
- Increase employee or customer retention
- Increase ability to pass a risk assessment
- Better end-to-end security or compliance solutions
- Enable the mobile/modern workforce
- Boost sales
- Enable quicker ROI
- Establish competitive differentiators
- Avoid obsolescence
- Implement best practices/standards
- Drive customer demand
- Increase demand gen

Conclusion

"Don't let the business run you...
Run your business." —Juan Fernandez

 When you understand how your product and services benefit your customer, and then work meaningfully together so technology becomes their competitive advantage, you won't have to have "cost conversations." You will already be generating money for them. They will see you as an essential piece of their business and a valuable partner who has a seat at the table.

It's time to stop selling products and instead start offering solutions to build and benefit your clients' businesses. Through *Quality* Business Reviews, you will soon be able to build your business and encounter a lot less complexity in your market space, which will unlock the door to everything.

Let's talk about how you can make your QBR part of your story so it can be impactful in presales and marketing.

Below is an exercise that will help you be successful delivering and having the conversations.

On a sheet of paper, mark off four quadrants, like the chart on the next page.

In the upper left section, outline your offering. This is "what you do."

In the upper right, make notes about how what you do is *different* from your competitors.

In the lower left, explain *why* your MSP's approach is so different.

Finally, in the lower right, make notes about the benefits or outcomes of your services.

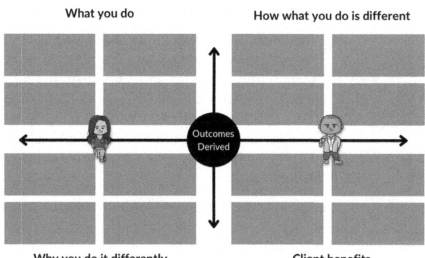

Your answers in each of these quadrants will serve as an outline for how to create branding and marketing messages that will laser target your ideal clients.

Marching Orders

It's time to build your (unpaid) sales force by creating raving fans. When you consistently deliver value to your clients, they will deliver referrals in turn. Focus on the referral-and-deliver service. Next thing you know, you will have a sales force paying you! When you empower your partners to be profitable, they will tell everyone!

RESOURCES

Pro tip! Don't stop here, Success is one click away...

Jump over and grab your free resources at:
theMSPhandbook.com

Here you will find activities, exercises, and additional education to drive goals and strategy with your clients, staff, and leadership.

Available free resources:

- A QBR template
- "The QBR your customer deserves"
- QBR SOP checklist from Team ELBO
- The Value Visualizer
- Needs, wants, fears exercise
- Know Your No
- Sample Risk Assessment
- Technology roadmap template
- And other great tools...

Contracts You Should Be Tracking:

- LOB Application Vendors
- Copier/Equipment Leases
- VolP & Telco Agreements
- Internet & Data Circuits
- Cloud (Azure, AWS, Google Cloud, etc.)
- Data Destruction (Shred & E-Waste)
- Web Hosting & Certificates
- Firewalls, Switches & Wireless Support & Maintenance
- Cameras, Door Access, HVAC & other IoT
- IT Training & SAT Subscriptions

Sample Agenda

1. Client Updates & Changes:

- What will change in the next 18 months?
- What is changing in your industry? (Commoditization, Growth, New Tech?)
- Is your business growing or shrinking?
  - Adding Employees or Locations?
  - New Technology?
  - Environment at a Glance
    - Asset Report Issues
    - User Report (If necessary)
    - Documentation Review
- What are 3 things you wish technology could do for you?

2. Relevant Updates from Previous QBR/Project Status

3. Goals/Themes Looking Ahead

4. Risk & Exposure Review: (45 min)

- Review Latest Risk Assessment
- Review Known Assets for:
  - Security Upgrades (out of date OS or vendor EOL)
  - Lifecycle Upgrades
- Present/Review Budget and Proposed Projects

Issues list: Identify, Discuss, Solve (30 min)

-
-
-

Wrap up: (5 min)

- Schedule next QBR
- Document new action items (to become tickets)
  - MSP Action Items:
    -
    -
  - Client To-Dos:
    -
    -

ACKNOWLEDGMENTS

The MSP community is built by so many caring and wonderful people and is truly an amazing place for learning and growth. We would be remiss if we didn't thank all our great friends, partners, and colleagues... and most importantly our wonderfully supportive family members. Our true gratitude goes out to all the amazing people who have contributed along the way.

(We might need another book just to appropriately recognize everyone. Maybe we will call it the *"Thank You Edition"*)

Thank you to the amazing leaders that gave their time to read and write the forewords in this book:

◊ Rob Rae, SVP of Business Development, Datto
◊ Arlin Sorensen, VP Ecosystem Evangelism, ConnectWise

To all the people who read the book in draft and helped to shape it:

◊ Alex Farling, Co-Founder and Channel Chief at Lifecycle Insights
◊ Ron Cotsopoulous, Operations Manager, Kobus Technologies

- ◊ Matt Elliott, Senior Solution Architect, LNS Solutions
- ◊ Matt Clarin, President, Hungerford Technologies
- ◊ Tricia King, Senior Consultant/vCIO, Vertikal6
- ◊ Kevin Elsing, Co-Founder and Vice President, Team ELBO
- ◊ William Pote, CEO, eTop Technology, Inc.
- ◊ Nigel Moore, CEO, The Tech Tribe
- ◊ Chris Wiser, CEO, 7Figure MSP
- ◊ Nick Coniglio, Co-Founder and Managing Partner, Lifecycle Insights

Extra special shout-outs to:

- ◊ Josie Stockman for her entertaining editing and visual graphic support!
- ◊ Demi Stevens for book badassery.
- ◊ Odom Sok, who turned us into illustrated characters and decided we needed a Bad Ass stance. We agree!

A huge thanks to our spouses and children for letting us spend weekend and evening time on this project.

And finally, thanks to you the reader. Together we can make a difference!

JUAN FERNANDEZ, CEO (aka The Chief Encouragement Officer) of MSP Growth Coalition, has built a scalable framework to empower business owners to scale. He recently hand built and architected the design of a multimillion-dollar MSP that consecutively ranked one of the fastest-growing IT companies in the industry.

The winner of *MSP Shark Tank* for best security and services presentation, this set the stage for an all-inclusive Security and Device as a service model that created a framework for channel and MSP models. He is also one of a select few to write the CompTIA A+, Network +, and Security + tests. He also sits on the CompTIA Subject Matter Expert Technical Advisory board.

Juan has been featured in *CompTIA World*, and *Channel Pro* magazines, named HP DaaS innovator of the year, awarded *CRN* magazine's Fastest Growing MSP, *ENX* magazine's Difference Maker of the Year, and is the 2022 Channel Influencer of the Year and *CompTIA*'s Industry Advisory Leadership Award winner.

MARNIE STOCKMAN, Ed.D., started her career in Customer Success with the toughest customers of all... high school math students. Her passion for education and using data and humor to help others grow and succeed took her from the classroom to Sr. Director of Customer Success of a leading Ed Tech company, and now to Co-Founder and CEO of Lifecycle Insights—a vCIO/Customer Success platform for MSPs. With her default setting locked on "smiles," she aims to create raving fans for Lifecycle Insights and help MSPs do the same for their customers.

Marnie can talk to a wall, but she would rather talk to a crowd. You can see her at industry events—sometimes presenting with Juan! She is featured on many podcasts, is a member of CompTIA's Channel Development Advisory Council, and is on the marketing committee for NSITSP.

She enjoys wrangling other vendors and MSPs in the space to engage in fun and educational content to help grow businesses. When she isn't Lifecycling, she can be found playing volleyball or golf with her husband and two 20-something kids in Greensboro, MD.

Made in the USA
Coppell, TX
30 July 2022

80621128R10066